Faith's

Motive

Faith's Motive

Ben Fisher

Why Publishing

Copyright © 2021 by Ben Fisher

All rights reserved. No part of this book may be reproduced in any manner whatsoever without written permission except in the case of brief quotations embodied in critical articles and reviews.

First Printing, 2021

ISBN: 978-1-8383531-4-8

Unless otherwise stated, Scripture quotations are from the ESV® Bible (The Holy Bible, English Standard Version®), copyright © 2001 by Crossway, a publishing ministry of Good News Publishers. Used by permission. All rights reserved.

Scripture quotations [marked NIV] taken from the Holy Bible, New International Version Anglicised Copyright © 1979, 1984, 2011 Biblica

Used by permission of Hodder & Stoughton Ltd, an Hachette UK Company.

All rights reserved.

'NIV' is a registered trademark of Biblica UK trademark number 1448790.

Faith's Motive

Introduction

This short book on Faith has been extracted and edited from a larger one: The Who and The Why, which looks at faith, hope and love together. In that book, I argue that the most helpful way to label these three attributes, so highly valued in the bible, is as 'motivational characteristics.' That is to say, that God wants to embed these three things at the core of our souls, to both define who we are, and motivate what we do. For it's not just what we do that's important, but why we do it. God has never been looking to simply change our actions, but rather to change us from the inside out – to alter our hearts and minds so that they naturally want and pursue all that is right and good. God is constantly working in His adopted children to conform them more and more to the likeness of His Son, Jesus Christ. But this doesn't mean He's out to make us all a bunch of clones. God is far too creative for that, and besides, the infinite worth and wonder of Christ could never be captured in any single one of us. But consistent throughout each and every one of us is God's desire to embed in the core of our being a faith, hope and love, which is both sourced and sustained in God alone. These three attributes are of eternal value and will remain as relevant in the next life as they are now. This book takes on the topic of faith, seeking to understand what it is exactly, how it affects us, and how we can work alongside God as He grows it within us.

Finding faith

So what exactly is faith? We use the word in a variety of ways, for example, we tend to mean something a little different when we say that someone is 'full of faith' as opposed to being 'faithful' (though they are strongly linked). We speak of 'The Faith' and 'blind leaps of faith'. Indeed people put their faith in a variety of things, be it the strength of the materials used in a building or a bridge they're crossing, or perhaps the competence of the people who designed and built it. We put our faith in businesses to do and carry out different tasks, like keeping us supplied with water and electricity or turning up when they say they will. We put our faith in our friends to be there when we need them. All these things are good, but they're not what we're talking about here. Just as it will be with hope and love, the faith we're talking about is a God-centered faith, and it should be no surprise that we'll find that for each of these the source is found in Him and that its presence in our lives will make our reflection of Him that little bit clearer.

In a film called Serenity, a kind of space/western written and directed by Joss Whedon, we find its main character, Mal, on the run from a sinister government agent. Mal flees to his old friend Shepherd Book, who has given Mal both advice and shelter in the past, only to find that Book and the children he looks after have been slaughtered. As Shepherd Book lays there dying he gives his final words of advice: "I don't care what you believe, just believe." In what is otherwise a well written film this key emotional moment falls a little flat because it simply just doesn't make sense. In fact the rest of the film shows exactly why: by this point much has already been made of how the unnamed agent 'believes hard' and part of his strength is in that. But his belief has clearly put him on the wrong side and led him to do awful things including the murder of Book and all those children. Furthermore, by the end, he comes to see how his faith has been misplaced in the regime he blindly and secretly upheld. So the film as a whole shows how silly such a comment truly is. Believing in something/anything is not what really matters. What matters is *what* we believe, or more to the point, who we put our faith in.

Now our base camp for exploring faith will be the well-known section from the book of Hebrews. From here we will gather a variety of things about the faith that God wants to infuse into us. It will not be exhaustive and there's much more that can be learned, but we will end up with a couple of simple truths that I believe helpfully summarise what faith in God looks like and the way that this God-centered faith affects and motivates us.

Assurance and Conviction

> *"Now faith is the assurance of things hoped for, the conviction of things not seen."*
>
> Hebrews 11:1

Straight away we hit something very important about faith but easily rushed over; faith is about assurance, substance, and conviction – certainty. In the world Faith can often be portrayed as an 'airy-fairy' type thing; "it's where (bless them) they believe (though there's no evidence) about something the rest of us clued up people don't..." But this is not how the Bible talks about faith, it uses words like conviction, or as some translations put it, evidence! Faith is the evidence of things not seen. We're not encouraged to believe in something, or indeed someone, with no evidence to support this belief. We hear the gospel about Jesus Christ, we read His Word and we are convicted to our core, we both see and hear the truth of what is being taught. We may not physically see God, but we can see evidence of Him literally everywhere. In Romans, Paul affirms that *"...His invisible attributes, namely, his eternal power and divine nature, have been clearly perceived, ever since the creation of the world, in the things that have been made."*[1] It's not just that through faith we can see this, but also that in our physical seeing and experience of creation our faith is affirmed and formed. And though many try to tell us otherwise it is all evidence of God.

Furthermore, when we come to faith in Christ, our faith is strengthened all the more as we find that we have *"received the Spirit of adoption as sons, by whom we cry, "Abba! Father!" The Spirit himself bears witness with our spirit that we are children of God."*[2] We may not be able to prove it to those around us, but to receive The Holy Spirit and have

1. Rom 1:20
2. Rom 8:15-16

His affirming presence in our lives is such great evidence of the reality of God that it can't help but build up our faith. It is all evidence, and it results in conviction and certainty in what is unseen. Or to put it another way - faith!

Miss-spelt?

At the time of writing I hadn't heard this said for quite a while, so hopefully it's been left behind now, but in the past, I've heard it said from quite a few places that "faith is spelt R.I.S.K." Now I understand why this is taught and there is a great golden nugget of truth in it, which we'll unpack later on in the book, but it's unhelpfully leaping ahead of itself. No, if anything faith is spelt S.U.R.E. Remember it's about certainty and conviction, and it's really important that we start with this.

The Core of the Matter:

> *"...without faith it is impossible to please him, for whoever would draw near to God must believe that he exists and that he rewards those who seek him."*
>
> Hebrews 11:5-6

Without faith it is impossible to please God. Just let that sink in a moment. Without faith you'll never please Him – it's simply impossible. And we're immediately told why, so the rest of that sentence is telling us key things about faith. Now I almost feel silly writing this as it's surely stating the obvious, but it's right there in the Bible to be said: a key part of faith is believing that God exists. It's as simple as that, and of course, you're not going to please anyone if you don't even acknowledge that they exist. But it's more than that, as James puts it in his letter *"Even the demons believe – and shudder!"*[3] Faith in God isn't just about believing that He exists but carries with it a desire to draw near to God, and a belief that there are rewards in seeking Him – that He is both worthy and worth it!

---

3. James 2:19

Jesus taught that:

> *"The kingdom of heaven is like treasure hidden in a field. When a man found it, he hid it again, and then in his joy went and sold all he had and bought that field."*
>
> *"Again, the kingdom of heaven is like a merchant looking for fine pearls. When he found one of great value, he went away and sold everything he had and bought it"*

Matt 13:44-46 NIV

And again:

> *"For which of you, desiring to build a tower, does not first sit down and count the cost, whether he has enough to complete it? Otherwise, when he has laid a foundation and is not able to finish, all who see it begin to mock him, saying, 'This man began to build and was not able to finish.'... So therefore, any one of you who does not renounce all that he has cannot be my disciple."*

Luke 14: 28-29,33

God is looking for people who believe in Him, and believe that there is reward in seeking Him. Not just any old reward, not something simply nice to have, but a reward of such worth and importance that we would give up anything and everything we have to get it.

At its core faith has a very simple message which it embeds and repeats over and over to our soul: *God is Greater!* This is why people become willing to give up so much for His sake, from simply giving up of their time to gather regularly with other Christian's, to giving up money and possessions to love and bless others, to even being willing to give up their life rather than deny the truth about God and His Son who died for us. Although there is so much more that can be said about faith, I believe this truly gets to the heart of the matter concerning what faith does in us, how it affects our character and motivates us.

The Cloud of Witnesses

So, continuing in the book of Hebrews and taking what we've learnt about faith, about certainty and greatness; let's see it in action - what does it look like to be a person motivated by faith? And we'll start with Abraham: "*By faith Abraham obeyed when he was called to go out to a place that he was to receive as an inheritance. And he went out, not knowing where he was going*"[4]. By faith Abraham obeyed. How easy and simple to say, yet how hard such obedience would be without faith. He didn't even have the vigour of youth on his side, he was 75 years old by now. He couldn't call ahead first and book himself a piece of land to stay in, he didn't hang around and make detailed plans, checking websites about Canaan, but rather he gathered his household and servants with all they had, and went. Why? Because he took God at His word. God told him to go, and promised to bless him. Indeed God promised to bless him and make him a blessing ultimately to the whole world!

That's quite a promise, and coming from anyone else would surely just be wind. Anyone could say those words, you probably hear politicians among others, regularly make high minded and well-intended promises about things they simply don't have enough control over or power to do. Even our better leaders can leave us disappointed with the results compared to the promises. But Abraham packed up and left not knowing what he was going to find, or what he was going to face in this new land. He could be certain of nothing, except of the one sending him – he was certain of the ability and character of God. And that's what faith allows us to

4. Heb 11:8

do too. It raises courage in us to step out when called by God, not knowing or being certain of all the details, but being certain of Him. *By faith Abraham obeyed.*

In turn, as God's promise to bless them started to take further shape, "*By faith Sarah herself received power to conceive, even when she was past the age, since she considered him faithful who had promised.*"[5] Humanly speaking what was promised to Sarah – to give birth to a child at her age, was not just unlikely or improbable, it simply was not going to happen without God's power at work. But thank God, His promises and callings come not with a boot out the door and some encouraging words, but rather they come with power and with His presence. I love the way that Matthew's gospel ends; with the command and call to go and make disciples of all nations, "*And behold, I am with you always, to the end of the age.*"[6] He doesn't say "now off you go, I'll see you at the end", but promises to be with them always. And we now know of course, that this promise was and is fulfilled through the receiving and the empowering of the Holy Spirit. God with, and in us!

For Sarah, her circumstances seemed to make it certain that she would never conceive, indeed to think otherwise was laughable. But Sarah became certain

5. Heb 11:11
6. Matt 28:20

of God over the circumstances, and so Isaac was born. It was God who chose his name, which in a lovely touch on His part means 'he laughs'. Indeed after his birth, Sarah said "God has made laughter for me…"[7]

I've got a great quote stuck up on my wall at home, taken from an article[8] by Jon Bloom about feeling unqualified for what God is calling you to do. I turn to it whenever I start to feel the weight of what I'm called to and my laughable inadequacy to achieve it. These kinds of feelings are quite normal and arguably appropriate. But only if it's backed up by the faith that God Himself will do it through us. So, in turn, I'm also reminded to take stock when I'm feeling a bit too sure of own abilities, and to humble myself afresh as I see my own meagreness, alongside how bountifully greater God is. It can be an uncomfortable thing to depend on someone else, to let go and entrust things to others. But what a release and a glorious weight is lifted as our faith grows more and more to know with certainty that God rules and reigns above all, without limit in knowledge, wisdom or power. And what He has promised, He will do. So let's remember, It was *by faith Sarah received power* to achieve the promise made to her.

---

7. Gen 21:6
8. 'Don't feel qualified for your calling?', Jon Bloom, DesiringGod.org

The Trial of Time

We should also consider another side to Abraham and Sarah's story, for though they are wonderful positive examples to us, the Bible is very honest about failures as well as triumph's in the lives of these witnesses. In Abraham and Sarah's case, the thing that weakened their faith is something that many, if not all followers of Jesus Christ have experienced – the trial of time. Or put another way, waiting for God to act. There were twenty-five years in total between God first promising to Abraham that he would have many descendants, being made into a great nation (and more), before the birth of Isaac.

That is a LONG wait, and it's this trial of time that has undone so many people, with Abraham and Sarah being no exception. Imagine it, Abraham is already seventy-five years old when he gets this promise and Sarah sixty-six. They were already considered past it in terms of having children. But to grow twenty-five years older as they wait for the promise to be fulfilled must have been incredibly difficult. I often think that patience is one of those things that you think you have until it's actually tested. It perhaps would not have been so bad if they'd been told from the beginning that it would take that long. You'd at least have a date to look towards and hold on to in your heart. But perhaps that's why God doesn't often give dates and times – because He wants us to learn to hold on to Him rather than a date? So when we learn that partway through this period, their faith wavered and they tried to make the promise happen in their own strength, we can be more than a little understanding, whilst hopefully learning from it and not making the same type of mistake in our own lives.

It was ten years into this period that they decided to take matters into their own hands. Sarah suggested to Abraham that he should sleep with her Egyptian servant called Hagar. And it worked? Well, Hagar conceived and had a child named Ishmael. But the two women from then on had contempt for each other, and the peace they had sought through trying to make God's promise happen through their own means resulted in nothing but strife and division within the camp. It was not an act of faith, and so came with none of faith's benefits or fruits. *Thankfully God is also greater than our failures, and our faithlessness.* God blessed and looked after Ishmael, and Abraham and Sarah still lived to see the child of promise born, in His timing and His way.

Promises, promises…

"By faith Isaac invoked future blessings on Jacob and Esau"[9] This is easily skipped over, indeed I had myself until someone pointed it out to me: he passed on or invoked future blessings. He passed on something he didn't physically have, just as Abraham had to him, and Jacob would to his sons – the promise that they would become a great nation and inhabit the land of Canaan. It would be a bit like me leaving in my will the promise of a million pounds to my children without actually having it (which I certainly do not), yet believing they would receive it. Madness? Wishful thinking? No, it was faith, because the person who had originally promised it is faithful. They had certainty that God was willing, able and eager to do it (in His timing). He had promised; therefore it would happen.

And don't all Christian parents want to be able to do this? To pass on their faith in the future blessings of being with Jesus Christ when He comes to reign once and for all time. When He makes a new heaven and earth which will never see sin! I know I do. I'm desperate that my girls will also receive this faith and the awesome future that comes with it. *By faith Isaac passed on future blessings.*

---

9. Heb 11:20

All of which leads us nicely onto our next example…

Home

"These all died in faith, not having received the things promised, but having seen them and greeted them from afar, and having acknowledged that they were strangers and exiles on the earth. For people who speak thus make it clear that they are seeking a homeland."[10] The truth is that as Christians we've never even seen let alone been to our home. That moment you were born again, made new, you became a stranger to the world you knew and you became an heir of the world to come. Do you feel that? Does the way you live reflect something of this truth? I know it's quite a challenge for myself. It's so easy to get caught up in investing in the here and now, and focusing only on what is in front of us. But it is a frequent trait found in those who are full of faith that their hearts are primarily set not on this life, but on the one to come.

We're sometimes told that 'home is where the heart is'. Well there's plenty of truth in that, and Jesus taught something very similar: that "…where your

---

10. Heb 11:13-14

treasure is, there your heart will be also."[11] We need to ask ourselves what is it we treasure most? Because what we treasure and put our time, effort and money into shows where our hearts truly are. If our hearts are genuinely set on God and the future life we will have with Him - faces unveiled, seeing Him unhindered and full of joyful awe – then there will be evidence now in how we live that demonstrates this is what we treasure most.

Let's consider one type of example: As I write this I have two daughters, aged four and almost three. They have many, many things. So many toys, which mummy and daddy are largely glad to give, and their grandparents are all the happier to give them. From our position as parents we've got to a place of wanting to be careful how much they get and how quickly, because it's so easy to just get more and more, and stuff our lives with so many little (or big) things, without appreciating or valuing them. You just move on to wanting the next thing. What's much more concerning (and annoying) about all this, is the realisation of how bad I can be, how easy it is for me to not appreciate what I have, and simply look to fill my own life with more stuff. I tell you, having children has been great for my walk with God thanks mostly to one key principle I've been trying to follow: Anything I get concerned or angry with my

11. Matt 6:21

children about, I ask God in what way I do the same type of thing with Him. It's been wonderfully humbling.

Now I'm not about to say that having anything other than the very bare essentials is bad and 'un-Christian'. But we do well to remember how Jesus encouraged His hearers not to build up their treasures on earth where it won't last, but instead to build up your treasure in heaven where they will last forever. How seriously we take these words of His will be a good measure of how much we're truly looking forward to our true home with God. These great witnesses of the Bible showed that they were certain of a greater time and place to come. Not by sitting around and without any care for this life, no, they got on with it, but with a heart attitude of belonging to another place and time. Feeling like foreigners passing through till the promised land is finally reached.

"If they had been thinking of that land from which they had gone out, they would have had opportunity to return. But as it is, they desire a better country, that is, a heavenly one. Therefore God is not ashamed to be called their God, for he has prepared for them a city."[12]

I'm finding more and more that as time goes on, I'm yearning for the day when I will never sin again.

12. Heb 11:15-16

Oh, I'm certain of Christ's sacrifice for me, that my debt is paid and I've been redeemed and saved from the punishment I deserved. I know I'm declared righteous before God because I am now *in* Christ who is truly righteous and holy. But in truth sin is still present in my life and I hate it. It brings me low and spoils to some level my relationship with everyone. Sin is a tiresome, enticing thing. But God has promised that when I'm raised again and given a new body I will be changed. Just as the power of sin over me was defeated at the cross, so the presence of sin in my life will be removed and finished with at Christ's return[13].

Now this longing in me, for my future sinless life with God is a comfort and encouragement to me, as it is, in itself, another sign of faith. These witnesses in Hebrews looked to and desired a better 'country' to come. But if they had wanted to, they would have been able to return to the land they'd come from. And it's the same with us, we are not forced to continue in a journey with God, we have the choice to return to the sins Christ died to save us from. It is a pitiful, lazy and poor choice to make, but one we are free to do. Oh, we all fail at times (daily – at least in my case), and each time it shows our imperfect faith. But praise God, Christ's blood remains more than enough to pay our debt of sin. Sadly, for some, sin remains too

[13]. 1 Cor 15:50-58

enticing and faith has not taken root in order to combat it and continually declare to their hearts that God is Greater! In the end, they do decide to return to 'the land' they had come from, abandoning Christ. Conversely, we're told that for those who want God, His ways and His ultimate plans, that God is not ashamed of them, not ashamed to be called their God. And has prepared a future life for them that will be better, that will be greater than they could even imagine.

Ask yourself honestly: where is home for you? What do you long for more? That which you find on this earth, or in the one to come? For if we're truly characterised and motivated by faith in God, it will affect our thinking and actions right here and now.

Greater than death

Well, we're not finished with Abraham quite yet. The Bible tells us of another event that's hard to even imagine. *"By faith Abraham, when he was tested, offered up Isaac."*[14] God told Abraham to sacrifice his son, Isaac. Now you've got to remember that Abraham had no idea that God would stop him

---

14. Heb 11:17

from doing it at the last moment. God had not yet revealed that He hates such practices[15], so there was no reason for him to think that he wouldn't have to go through with it. What was going through his mind as he led Isaac up that mountain? Well, the account in Genesis doesn't say, but Hebrews does: *"He considered that God was able even to raise him from the dead"*[16]. What faith! He considered, he reasoned, and came to the conclusion that the God who made the entire universe and who sustains all things, who had seen them through their troubles, who had always done exactly as He said He would, who had promised that through Isaac, Abraham would have more descendants than grains of sand on the seashore – well then surely this same God will do something to make sure His promise is fulfilled. And he reasonably concluded that the only way God could do that is by bringing Isaac back to life. It's entirely logical. But only if you first understand who Abraham was dealing with. Knowing what He did about God, it was both reasoned and reasonable to go ahead and sacrifice his son believing that he would receive him back from the dead. *By faith Abraham, when he was tested, offered up Isaac.*

Before moving on, let's just take a moment to consider why God even did this. Why would God feel the need to test Abraham's faith? He's the God who

15. Lev 18:21
16. Heb 11:19

knows the secrets and motivations of our hearts, who has known our every thought and action we'll ever make from before we were born. He already knows exactly what we'll do and why in every given situation. In Genesis we're told: *"He said, "Do not lay your hand on the boy or do anything to him, for now I know that you fear God."*[17] In what way did God now know that Abraham feared Him, that He didn't before? In experience. And this episode in Abraham's life shows us that seeing in action, and experiencing our faith at work is important to God, beyond simply knowing that we would act in faith if challenged to. It also tells us that another outworking of faith will be a motivation to fear God.

Worthy of greater fear

"By faith Noah, being warned by God concerning events as yet unseen, in reverent fear constructed an ark for the saving of his household." [18] The fear of God is one of those things that tends to be taken to extremes by the church as a whole. Where it's either overemphasised, and everyone is encouraged to do as they're told lest they be sent to hell, or in the other extreme, which seems more

---

17. Gen 22:12
18. Heb 11:7

common in our age, there can be a distinct lack of any fear or reverence towards God. If it's overemphasised, often no time is given to the love and grace of God, that woos and encourages His people towards the better life He wants for them, picking us up when we fall. Nor indeed to the help He wants to give through the empowering of The Holy Spirit. Where it's under emphasised, people strive forwards to take seriously the good and nice promises of God in the Bible, but fail to take seriously and maybe even proactively ignore the warnings given by the same God in the same Bible. We must for our own sake, cherish and hold up high both the kindness and severity of God as Paul puts it,[19] not simplifying our God and His character – a sad and dangerous thing to do. Faith can help us with this, as it did with Noah. There was no sense in Noah that God wouldn't actually wipe out the rest of humanity; no questioning how a God of love could do such a thing. He took God at His word and believed what He said. Both in terms of the coming judgement and what Noah needed to do save himself and his family. It must have seemed crazy to those who knew him, spending who knows how long to construct a huge boat, far away from the sea in the belief that a flood, of indeed biblical proportions, was on its way from God! But he was carried along by faith, by certainty

---

19. Rom 11:22

in the One who had warned him. Then in turn through a healthy, reverent fear of God. Noah knew to take God seriously when all those around him saw no reason to honour God at all.

Now don't go thinking that the God of the Old and New Testaments are different God's or that He's mellowed since the Old Testament times. He is the One and only true God, the same yesterday, today and forever. Unchanging in character or substance. That's why He's so dependable and unfalteringly true to His word and Himself. That's why we can trust Him entirely. We may now know and experience His love in ways that weren't fully revealed during Old Testament times, but remember, the way this is most fully expressed with Christ Jesus, His sacrificial death and glorious resurrection, was all planned from before the creation of the world. It's hinted at, foreshadowed and even foretold in so many ways in the Old Testament. The plan never changed, and God never changed.

So now, coming back the other way we must realise that the God we meet in the Old Testament is still the same God we encounter in the New Testament, not to mention in our daily lives now. The God of Noah, who justly judged the whole earth and decided to save a select few, is our very same God today. Remember all those people deserved to die in that way – God wasn't having a bad day, He was acting with complete justice, and one day He will judge the entire earth again. A day has been set when Christ will return to judge the living and the dead. This day will come – it's unavoidable, and is getting ever closer. The consequences of this judgement day will be utterly just, eternally lived with, and beyond our imagination - whether for the good or bad.

Now we have no ark to build, and no way to save ourselves. Instead, we have one provided: we're told that in repenting and believing in Christ and what He did for us, in being baptised in His name, we are now found *in Him* if we continue in our faith. Jesus Christ, He is our ark to save us from the wrath of God. We are now covered and credited with Christ's righteousness, His goodness, and furthermore have the Holy Spirit dwelling in us, changing us from the inside. God surrounding us, and God living inside us. Praise God, He is very thorough in His saving plan. And just like Noah, we'll have plenty of people mocking us for what we do and believe. They'll see no reason to prepare for a future judgement before the Lord of All. Noah could have given in to the sneering of others he must have experienced. After all, it's the easier thing to do. It would have taken a long time and a lot of effort to build the ark, plenty of time to question what on earth He was doing: was it really necessary or worth it? Will God truly do such a thing? But Noah didn't give in or hold back. He was carried along by a healthy, reverent fear of God, born in faith. And through this faith he saved both himself and his household.

Furthermore, Christ told His listeners: "do not fear those who kill the body but cannot kill the soul. Rather fear him who can destroy both soul and body in hell."[20] This is quite a stark statement that can't faithfully be softened. For some Christians around the world, this is sadly and immediately relevant – those whose lives are genuinely in danger because of their faith in Jesus Christ. As it stands, many Christians aren't facing that kind of physical threat at the moment, but this teaching remains just as relevant. For if it applies to physical beatings, surely it must apply to verbal ones. How tempting it is to shrink back when we need to openly stand up for Christ, displaying our faith in Him through our words and actions. And all because we fear what others might say to us, or even simply about us. It's such a dishonour to God when we let fear get the better of us in this way, and shows a distinct lack of faith. This is not the outworking of a soul believing and continually discovering that God is greater in every way and over every circumstance. By shrinking back we're treating God as being of less worth than the

20. Matt 10:28

people we're fearing. But good news - a faith born fear of God can release us from a fear of others. Far from being a bad thing, it is a blessing and a release, and personally, I desire to have more of it imbedded in my soul through faith in Him. *By faith Noah... in reverent fear constructed an ark for the saving of his household.*

The Golden Nugget

Now we turn to the story of Shadrach, Meshach and Abednego, who are surely in mind when the author of Hebrews refers to those who "*quenched the power of fire.*"[21] And it's here that we to return to the risk theme briefly mentioned earlier, in order to find that golden nugget of truth. Faith is not about risk. But it does provide a great foundation from which to take one. Shadrach, Meshach and Abednego (or Hananiah, Mishael and Azariah as they were originally known) were among the first group of Jews to be deported to Babylon. They along with Daniel were picked out to be trained as potential advisors to the king of Babylon - Nebuchadnezzar. Through God's blessing and anointing on their life's they proved to be among the best, most helpful advisors

21. Heb 11:19

he had. What could have been going through their heads? They endured so much change, having been captured and taken to an unfamiliar land, not knowing what to expect, and then ended up possibly in an even more privileged position than they'd had before in Judah?

But this did not spare them from coming into conflict with a king who thought far too highly of himself. Nebuchadnezzar had a huge golden image of himself made, and I mean huge! The Bible records it as sixty cubits high, or in more modern measurements about twenty-seven meters. That's between three to four times higher than the height of the average house in the UK. Now when the music played everyone was required to bow down and worship the image. I like to imagine the king watching people walk along going about their daily lives and trying to order the music to start at awkward moments to catch people out. Almost like a game of musical chairs/bowing where the last one standing has to sit at the side and they move onto the next round? But disappointingly it wasn't like that at all, and to remain standing wasn't to lose a game but to lose your life. Nevertheless, these three men of faith remained standing. The result was to be brought before the king who gave them one last chance to bow before his golden image and worship it…

"Shadrach, Meshach and Abednego replied to him, "King Nebuchadnezzar, we do not need to defend ourselves before you in this matter. If we are thrown into the blazing furnace, the God we serve is able to deliver us from it, and he will deliver us from Your Majesty's hand. But even if he does not, we want you to know, Your Majesty, that we will not serve your gods or worship the image of gold you have set up."

Dan 3:16-18 NIV

At first, it reads like they are absolutely certain that God will save them, and then they throw in a 'but': "*But even if he does not...*" They're not doing this because they know for sure God will save them (although they do seem fairly confident), but the point is they see God as worth dying for. Their faith, their certainty, is in a God both able to save, and who is worth surrendering their lives to, even if that means being burned alive. And so, from this rock-solid foundation, they are compelled to launch off and take the risk. I love how the whole thing comes across as being done in a calm, polite, matter-of-fact boldness.

Let's take another example of *faith-inspired* risk, featuring Jonathan (King Saul's son), and his armour bearer. I really like Jonathan's story. He seems to have been a genuinely good man and full of faith in God. It's a real shame his father wasn't more like him. Now on this particular occasion Jonathan and his armour bearer are out on their own and heading towards one of the Philistine's garrisons:

> *Jonathan said to his young armour-bearer, "Come, let's go over to the outpost of those uncircumcised men. Perhaps the Lord will act in our behalf. Nothing can hinder the Lord from saving, whether by many or by few."*

>> 1 Sam 14:6 NIV

"Perhaps the Lord will act". PERHAPS! Again, we've got the solid foundation of faith: *"nothing can hinder the LORD from saving by many or by few"*, the certainty that their God is greater than the Philistines, which provides the launch pad from which to take a risk: *"It MAY BE that the LORD will work for us"*. That's quite a risk, two people up against a garrison of the enemy. We have no idea how many people were in that garrison, only that they killed about twenty in the first strike[22]. And it wasn't just Jonathan who was full of faith: *"...his armour-bearer said to him, "Do all that is in your heart. Do as you wish. Behold, I am with you heart and soul."*[23] Really? I've got to admit my response may well have

---

22. 1 Sam 14:14
23. 1 Sam 14:7

been more like: 'Well yes He *can* save with just the two of us, but wouldn't it be sensible to go and get a few (hundred) others?'

Both these stories have great outcomes and the hero's faith is rewarded straight away. But what if they hadn't? What if instead, we read of how Shadrach, Meshach and Abednego died in the flames refusing to bow down to the golden image, and of how Jonathan and his armour bearer died valiantly but needlessly attacking a garrison on their own? Would their stories be any less faith-filled? No of course not! Not so inspiring admittedly. But God loves to respond to faith because it pleases Him so much. And if not in this life, certainly in the life to come they would have received their reward. These stories, these lives, displayed something of God's worth, glory, and faithfulness, to all those who saw it happen.

So, remember faith is not about risk. But maybe, it might just motivate you to take the risk of your life, for the glory of God? Or perhaps more simply speaking up and taking the risk of being rejected or ridiculed for Jesus' sake? Because behind it all you have this certainty, this faith – that God is worth it. That He is greater.

Beyond the cloud

"And what more shall I say? For time would fail me to tell of..."[24] So much could be said about each person and line written, but much like the writer of Hebrews did, I'm hitting a point where it feels right to move on. Beyond this great cloud of witnesses is the God-Man Himself. To follow their example our primary focus needs to be on Christ, not them. He's the one to set our sights on, and where our faith finds both its source and destination. He showed the way by doing what He did for the joy set before Him. Not duty, but joy. He too looked to the reward and found it greater.

Now we're encouraged to run our race, our life of faith, with endurance (we need to keep going, it's not going to be over quickly). And to do this well, we need to untangle ourselves from every "weight and sin"[25]. I don't care how good an athlete you might be, if you go into a race with a rope tied around you attached to stones, even if small stones, you're going to be held back from doing your best. And if they're too big you're going to be held back from moving at all!

Consider how faith in Christ changes how we relate to sin. No matter how badly you fell, or how deep you went into the abyss of sinfulness, Christ's

24. Heb 11:32
25. Heb 12:1

sacrifice on the cross was greater, and His power over death was greater so that the grave could not hold Him down. As the earlier parts of the book of Hebrews tells us; Christ is a better mediator, a better High Priest of a better covenant, with a better message. He didn't just pay the penalty of our sins, He went beyond that, and now we who believe in Him have credited to our account His righteousness. You may have heard this helpful way of remembering what justification or being justified means. You break up the word to *Just As If I'd…* never sinned. But more than that, better than that, through Christ it's *Just As If I'd…* lived the perfect life of Christ. We go from having an unpayable debt, not to breaking even, but to being credited with something we could never earn. From God's enemies to God's adopted children. God's plan and means of salvation was and is so much greater than we could have ever dreamed up.

But there's more. In our on-going battle with sin in our lives, faiths internal whisper of encouragement – that He is greater, now starts to provide a more meaningful alternative in every situation, along with the power to follow it.[26] You see, so often, instead of simply trying harder when faced with any given temptation, what we need instead is to cultivate a superior desire – something even better to chase after.

26. 1 Cor 10:13

Jesus didn't come to give us a better rule book to live by, He came to bring freedom, to release us into fulness of life! So to address greed He says to His disciples, "*Do not lay up for yourselves treasures on earth, where moth and rust destroy and where thieves break in and steal, but lay up for yourselves treasures in heaven, where neither moth nor rust destroys and where thieves do not break in and steal.*"[27] Reminding them also that this is a sign of where their heart truly is. Sadly there are far too many people both inside and outside the church who seem to think that following Christ is about denying yourself. And it is, but this is only half of the message! And a half-truth can be wholly false. We deny ourselves in order to go after what is better. The rewards of which may or may not be found directly in this life. In some ways, we'll discover the blessing of living as God wants us to right here and now, discovering that (wouldn't you know it), God really does know what He's talking about. And in some ways, we'll be like Abraham and the others on this list, who see the promise from afar, but will have to wait till Christ returns to receive the prize of our faith.

Another example of seeking this greater desire is found when Paul, briefly addressing drunkenness, encourages his readers to go on being filled with the Holy Spirit rather than filling themselves up on

27. Matt 6:19-21

wine.[28] Now wine, of course, is not bad in and of itself, and Jesus Himself enjoyed it with His disciples. But so many have turned to wine and alcohol in its different forms to find escape from the mundane or grim parts of life. However, it is no saviour, and so often brings out the worst in people. The encouragement brought, is to seek to be filled with Him who empowers, brings love and fullness of life. Who brings out the very best in people.

Now it's not just the bad, but some good stuff can weigh us down too. God may well require of you to give up things perfectly fine in and of themselves, but that are getting in the way of your relationship with Him or the direction He has for you in life. I'll give you a couple of examples from my life. Firstly, games. I have at different times become quite addicted to different games on my mobile phone. Things that started as just a helpful five minute distraction or wind down from time to time, became all-consuming and started to occupy far too much of my time and thoughts. Several times over the years, God has spoken to me about putting a game down because of this. And each time I would, then months later I'd start on a new game. At first, all would be well, and it wouldn't consume me, indeed it would be a genuinely helpful occasional distraction. Then I'd start turning to it more and more till it occupied time

28. Eph 5:18

that I might otherwise have spent speaking with God or thinking about His word. So for me, I've needed to put them down completely, as something that hinders more than helps me. Now there's nothing intrinsically wrong with playing games on your mobile, and for you, it's probably no issue at all? But if like me you know that it absorbs your time and mind more than is helpful, it's time to delete that game. Right now. You may not want to, but trust me it will do you good (as long as you don't fill that space in your life with something equally unhelpful. Been there. Done that).

Another example from my life concerns a hobby of mine. Like many people, I enjoy experimenting with food. I love to play with different flavours and methods, and come up with new dishes to enjoy with family and friends. I do this far less often now we have kids, but it's still something I find time to do, which I like to think I bless others with too (though they may just all be very polite). Not long ago I had an idea that would allow me to branch out into a completely new area: I had an inspiration for how I'd like to make and flavour my very own chocolate bar. I had discovered that they make small worktop chocolate refiners for people interested in giving it a go. It wasn't a completely silly price for me to consider, and I could probably save up for it over a year or two. However, praying one morning God simply told me to put the idea down, as it would be a distraction from what He has for me to do. Not that it was a bad thing, but rather a weight that would tangle me up and hinder me in my race at this time. So I did. It was a little disappointing of course, and I don't know the exact why, but it would be far worse not to listen to God's guidance and so miss out in other more important ways. Far worse still, would be to not listen and obey in this tiny little thing, where God spoke so clearly to me. I don't know about you, but if I find people aren't listening to me, I become less inclined to put much effort into speaking to them?

Whatever 'weight' it might be that God wants you to drop, it will require faith to do it. Once again, it's about that whisper being repeated from the core of your soul – "it's worth it because He is greater."

Help my unbelief!

Perhaps the best news to discover amongst all this, is that God is also greater than our faith, or lack of. God does and always has started with us where we are, and continues with us every step of the way. Continuously moulding and shaping us like the master craftsman He is, giving us opportunity after opportunity to grow in faith. Jesus once met a man whose child was seized by an evil spirit. This spirit had made the boy mute and frequently caused him to convulse and foam at the mouth, which happened in Jesus' presence. It had been a problem since childhood and had sometimes cast the boy into either flames or water to try and kill him.[29] The disciples had been trying to cast the evil spirit out but without success. Then Jesus came on the scene, and the child's father turned to Him saying *"If you can do anything, please have compassion on us and help us."*[30] If? Jesus didn't seem very impressed with this. If? Of course, I can, He says, anything is possible for one who believes! The response of this father was wonderfully honest and perhaps contained a little more faith than we tend to give him credit for: *"I believe: help my unbelief!"*[31] And there, in a nutshell, we have one of our common problems: so often we're operating out of a mixture of faith and unbelief. There's so much going on inside us most of the time, some good, and some bad. But Jesus didn't turn away saying come back when you believe without any doubt. To be sure there were times when Jesus said he couldn't perform many miracles in a place because of their lack of faith[32]. And I don't think we should take that as being physically incapable. He could still

29. Mark 9:14-29
30. Mark 9:22
31. Mark 9:24
32. Matt 13:58

do what He wanted as the all-powerful Son of God. But rather because He only did what He saw His Father doing[33], what His Father wanted, and His Father wants to respond to and reward faith. And that's exactly what He did here. He responded to an imperfect but visible faith. Indeed, in the very words 'help my unbelief' the child's father was actually displaying some faith. It was right there in his appeal to Jesus for help. The father could see that there was reason to believe, but his weak and very human soul just wasn't fully there. He needed help, just like we all do at times, and he was asking just the right person. This small, weak, act of faith was enough because it still looked to God and honoured Him as the one capable of making the difference, the one who was greater than his unbelief.

In Matthew's Gospel, we're told of another detail about this event. After the boy had been released, the disciples asked Jesus why they were unable to cast out the evil spirit. This was a new experience for them. Jesus had already been sending them out in twos to heal the sick, cast out demons, teach repentance and about the kingdom of heaven.[34] Jesus responded to them saying *"Because you have so little faith. Truly I tell you, if you have faith as small as a mustard seed, you can say to this mountain, 'Move from here to there,' and it will*

33. John 5:19
34. Mark 6:7-13

move. Nothing will be impossible for you."[35] This has not tended to encourage me. My initial internal response to this is normally: 'If faith the size of a mustard seed can do that – just how small and pathetic is mine?!" It's a strong challenge, and one I shouldn't just brush aside. But maybe there's a bit more going on here as well? There's another place in Matthew's gospel where Jesus uses the image of a mustard seed to describe the kingdom of heaven. Here He speaks of how this seed that starts off so tiny, grows into a tree larger than all the other plants in the garden.[36] So maybe alongside the challenge to my lack of faith, should also be the encouragement of potential? This seed of faith within me, that has already grown some, still has every possibility of growing into something much bigger and potent. And there's another thing to remember; as we considered at the beginning of the book, the primary and most important thing about faith is who or what you're putting it in. If our faith is in God, the Awesome Lord of All, who made the universe and all that's in it. Who loves to respond to people's faith in Him – well then even imagination can't limit what is possible through Him. As is so often the case, it comes back to a simple truth: We are weak, and He is strong. Thank God it's not primarily about us.

35. Matt 17:20
36. Matt 13:31-32

Faith

So now we come to the end of this little book on faith, and we ask: What does it look like to be a person characterised and motivated by faith? This person will know with certainty, from the core of their being, that God exists. That He is good. That He wants us to have a relationship with Him, and that He is worth pursuing above all else, because quite simply, He is greater. This will be displayed in every area of our lives, from our hidden thoughts to our words, and perhaps most strikingly our choices and actions. More and more we'll find that we're not hindered or motivated by fear of others or anything else, but that we're freed by a faith born fear of God, and a faith born desire for God. Where our every deed shows that we want and cherish God and His ways, above anything and anyone else. Would you like this to be a good description of you? I know I would.

Other books in this series:

Hope's Motive:

Often used merely to describe our wishes or optimism; other times expressed in ways that make it indistinguishable from faith. But hope has its own unique and vital function, raising our sight and bringing God centred anticipation.

Hope is the lifter of these.

Other books in this series:

Love's Motive:

Neither merely a feeling nor simply a choice that you make. Love is a motive and the way in which we place true value in other people.
Sourced and sustained in God, the beauty of this gift defies description, yet inspires us to try.

Love is the greatest of these.

www.ingramcontent.com/pod-product-compliance
Lightning Source LLC
Chambersburg PA
CBHW071546080526
44588CB00011B/1814